Flower Sense

Flower Sense

The Art of Decorating with Flowers

Tricia Guild

Photographs by James Merrell

Text by Elspeth Thompson with Tricia Guild

RIZZOLI
NEW YORK

Contents

Introduction 6

City 8

Vintage 24

Modern 40

Romantic 56

Party 72

Country 88

Exotic 104

Minimal 120

Garden 136

Working with flowers 152

Stockists 158

Acknowledgments 160

Flowers have a language and essence of their own. I have always been touched by the purity and spirit of this language and try to absorb their essence into my life and work. Looking, sensing, and trying to understand one of earth's miracles brings further questions and allows me to learn more. As a designer, I give flowers a crucial role in my creative process, which provides inspiration for patterns and colors. And at home, where I grow them in my gardens, both in London and in Italy, flowers are a constant presence around the house, transforming rooms with their beauty, style, warmth, and feeling.

The more I learn about flowers, the more I appreciate their purity. They do not need to be displayed in elaborate

Introduction

Tricia Guild

arrangements. On the contrary, just a few blooms, well chosen and thoughtfully placed, have the power to change the balance of an interior, to create different moods, and to delight the spirit. Time taken on flowers is never wasted. Selecting, arranging, and caring for them is, for me, one of life's most beautiful and rewarding rituals.

These pages are my personal homage to flowers. I hope to share my love of them, my respect for them, and the creative spirit with which I try to respond to their miraculous colors, shapes, and scents. Whether the end result is romantic or rustic, modern, minimal, or exotic, the same loving care and fascination lie behind every vase.

City

Flowers bring a city home to life, providing a vital connection with wild nature and the changing seasons. Buying fresh flowers every week from the florist's or market and bringing them home to arrange around the house is a life-enhancing ritual that gives meaning and joy to urban living. There's no such thing as a "city flower." Although it's true that some of the more architectural shapes and strong colors favored by stylish florists can lend an air of urban sophistication to both period and modern interiors, garden flowers such as peonies and snowballs can look equally at home. It's more about the way that the flowers are used—bringing some of the wit, style, and sophistication that make city life all over the world so alluring and exciting.

At home in London, I change the mood and feel of the rooms with different flowers. There is color in this living room, and fresh flowers can accentuate the color, contrast with it, or calm the atmosphere. At one end of the room, the bright accent colors of the cushions and other furnishings have been used in the flowers—a mixture of garden and florist's blooms as gloriously eclectic and unexpected as city life itself. It is creative finding new ways to use classic favorites. Peonies—for some the quintessential country flower—are seldom displayed individually on long stems with architectural alliums or nerines. Or, for a different but equally strong look, cut the cleaned stems to six inches and plunge them into a low bowl—the mass of papery petals has a wonderful air of opulence, and on a practical note, the heavy blooms will be less likely to droop.

At the other end of the living room, I can create a cooler, calmer mood by restricting the colors of the flowers to lilac

and lime green on a green glass table. Spotted banda orchids, the epitome of city chic, are mixed with pretty garden

flowers such as hyacinths, bluebells, sweet peas, and delphiniums—all given a modern urban spin in a collection of

frosted and plain glass vases, with just a few stems in each. On the table, a selection of flower heads nipped at the

top of the stems—peonies, pink nerines, carnations, delphiniums, and green snowballs—look fantastic floating in a

shallow dish of water. This is also a good way to use the remaining good blooms in an arrangement that is fading.

People lucky enough to have a small city garden in which to gather a few flowers for the house can bring the outside in.

Sculptural blooms, such as bearded iris and tulips, are particularly suited to city interiors, as their silky textures and subtly

patterned petals have a sensuous and sophisticated vitality. Display them singly, or in minimal groups in heavy, hand-

blown bowls and vases, to allow them to be seen in all their glory. A few leaves from the garden border provide the

perfect accompaniment: fresh green frothy alchemilla, the acid lime of golden hops, or a single spearhead frond of

Arum italicum.

Create an indoor urban woodland
with twiggy branches, spires of
delphinium, and dangling garlands
of hyacinth bells—as densely blue
as bluebells.

With their graphic shapes and unexpected colors, dahlias are a natural choice for the urban interior. Here in this modern city loft, they are perfectly complemented by the chunky shapes and rich jewel colors of the glass vases and tea glasses—the posies of blooms are given a quirky touch with a few lupin leaves and some spindly stems of white chincherinchees for height. The colors refer back to the fabrics and furnishings in a wonderfully rich layering of pattern on pattern.

Some flowers are famously ephemeral—Icelandic poppies live out their brief but beautiful lives in the space of a few days. It is a joy to watch the fat, hairy buds swell and open, spilling out crinkled papery petals in citrus shades that frill themselves in the warmth. Accentuate the kinks in the stems—keep them long, in a tall glass vase with just one ramrod-straight allium or chincherinchee—and let the colors sing out in style against a contrasting plain backdrop.

It is fun to display familiar flowers in a completely new way. Take this mass of half-open daffodils in a plain glass ice bucket: With stems tightly trussed, without leaves, and laid on the slant, they are suddenly sculptural, modern, and urban—a far cry from Wordsworth's dancing golden clouds. And yet, against the fresh lime green walls, the intensity of yellow is like a splash of country sunshine in the heart of the city.

Vintage

Timeless yet contemporary, the vintage look for interiors has never been so fashionable. And there are plenty of flowers that are the perfect complement for treasures and trinkets from times gone by. Roses are a great choice—not the blowsy old-fashioned types, but the tight pointed buds and pristine blooms of candy pink hybrid teas, with all their associations of 1950s glamour. Camellias, with their glossy leaves and waxy pastel petals, have a movie-star charm, harking back to the 1940s—a single bloom in a small vase could be waiting to be plucked for a corsage on a ball gown. Peonies seem straight from a vintage print, while whorls of ranunculus petals look as if they have been cut from the softest silk; don't confine them to vases, but use them in other witty and unexpected ways.

Vibrant color and quirky touches bring the elegant period features of this bedroom to life. Confining the color scheme to pinks would have been less fun; and here, the mass of orange ranunculus—stalks cut short and crammed into a chinoiserie-style cup and saucer—are a welcome surprise. Decadent details give the room the seductive air of a boudoir. In front of the fire, garlands made from white tuberose, ranunculus, and peonies are hung like floral necklaces, while scent—the ultimate seductress—hangs heavy in the air.

Taking its cue from the collection of vintage prints and other framed pictures above the fireplace, the color scheme for the flowers in this bedroom is an unusual mix of muted mauves, offset with white and fresh lime green. Arranged in sparse, asymmetric nosegays along the mantelpiece (see also previous page), or singly in tiny clear glass vases just a few inches high, Victorian favorites—such as roses, pansies, fritillaries, and lily of the valley—are given a fresh, contemporary twist.

Mixing periods and types of flower keeps things fresh: On a vintage Italian table by the window, dark dusky bells of *Fritillaria persica* are paired with white Solomon's seal and apple blossom in a 1950s vase, while pink sweet peas look pretty in a lusterware teacup with a single hosta leaf laid alongside. Sweet peas, with their frilled and fragrant petals, have an old-fashioned charm, and the brownish bells of the fritillaries are suffused with Victorian melancholy. At the same time, these little arrangements have a wit and grace that bring them right up-to-date.

As decorative as tasseled vintage bellpulls, garlands of white hyacinth bells and pale pink roses hang from the chandelier in this ultrafeminine living room. Sprays of cherry, pear, and hawthorn blossom are fresh and prettily nostalgic alongside peonies, rosebuds, and the occasional dark pink primula. Bring branches of spring blossom inside while they are still in bud; the flowers will soon open in the warmth and fill the room with their fragile, ephemeral beauty—then save tiny sprigs that fall to tuck into smaller vases.

Bearded iris, single
white peony, frilled
double peony,
Solomon's seal,
and a lacy froth
of dill.

Modern

Flowers are neither modern nor old-fashioned in themselves, but some have certain associations. Violets and hydrangeas, for instance, seem to hark back to Victorian times—but surely that's a cue to reinvent them, with minimal styling and contemporary containers. Any flower can look modern if used in the right way. The key lies in keeping things simple. This doesn't mean minimal: some of the following arrangements are actually quite elaborate. But if you are using many different flowers, or many little arrangements, do cut down on color—just one or two at the most, with possibly a contrasting accent. And it helps to keep the silhouette clear, clean, and graphic. Flowers rise to their setting, of course, and that includes contemporary containers, as well as the fabric and furnishings of the room.

There were already accents of red in my London studio, mainly in the collection of contemporary ceramics and Perspex and glass vases. Taking the color cue from these items for the flowers has given this light, modern space a heightened energy and vitality. Dahlias in different shades of red, from scarlet to dark crimson, have a stylized graphic quality that looks instantly modern, especially when stripped of their leaves. Instead of being massed in one large bunch, the flowers have been arranged in ones and twos throughout the room.

Proof that you don't have to be minimal to be modern, these pretty garden flowers are arranged in a contemporary style. Massed together, the alliums, iris, wisteria, hyacinths, and rosebuds would look countrified and romantic. Instead, they are divided into contrasting shapes and heights and displayed for maximum graphic impact. Alternating erect bearded irises with drooping fronds of wisteria along the mantelpiece is an original touch, as is cutting just one allium head short, so it nestles in the top of a vase of taller blooms.

A tabletop is a blank canvas waiting to be transformed with flowers and foliage, ceramics and glass. This one has a reflective green glass surface, which adds an extra layer of richness to whatever is placed on it. When setting the table for lunch or dinner, I keep the arrangements low, so the guests can see each other, but at other times I enjoy using tall stems such as those of fennel, snowball, and sculptural bells of Ireland.

Keeping to a strictly green and white color scheme is a strong statement in a green-painted room with views out across the green garden. The effect is to throw all the contrasting shapes and textures of the flowers, leaves, and stems into sharp relief—the arching stems of bells of Ireland, the milky green froth of snowballs, and the crisp, glistening purity of Amazon lily. Glass containers—vintage Memphis pieces, chunky clear bowls, and green wine glasses—coupled with the reflective glass of the table, give the arrangement a shimmering, multilayered look.

The collection of contemporary glass and ceramics on my studio shelves is not always filled with flowers. Each piece is strongly sculptural in its own right, needing no further adornment. But from time to time the addition of a few carefully chosen flowers allows them to be seen in a new light. Matching the blooms with the right receptacle took some experimenting: just one tall pink nerine and a few viola leaves in the red and clear Perspex vase; a crimson peony head and spray of green guelder rose in the squat ceramic pot; and a mass of pink peony and carnation petals in the Salviati glass bowl. It was hard to find something for the scarlet ceramic dishes because of their sculptural curves and deep gloss finish, but in the end, a single striped red and white rose and a sprig of snowball put the final touch to this modern still life.

This elegant period room has already been given a contemporary feel with wallpaper and furnishings that are a modern take on the classical. The flowers take the look further, with a spirited mix of bright pink nerine lilies and peonies, with contrasting green foliage and touches of pale pink and white. Clear glass vases are ranged along the mantelpiece, while on the table, handmade Salviati vases knit together the colors and forms of flowers, foliage, and furnishings. The addition of just one scarlet single peony head throws the scheme pleasantly off-center.

Romantic

All flowers are romantic. From time immemorial, all cultures have used them to say "I love you," to decorate weddings, and to mark anniversaries. It is hard to imagine a setting for romance without flowers. Roses, lilies, and violets are traditionally thought of as romantic, but individual flowers can form their own more personal associations—for some people it may be bluebells from a long-remembered walk, or the heady, seductive scent of tuberose. Romance is all about mood and atmosphere—soft colors, delicate textures, and the feeling that time and trouble have been taken to create something special. When it comes to flowers, this may mean tiny bedside posies of violets, pink-tinged rosebuds in gilded teacups, or even delicate garlands of fragrant hyacinth bells. Flowers such as these have the power to open a closed heart.

Many people associate pink with romance, but for me it's the color blue. The soft-textured blue on my bedroom walls has a lot of red in it, which makes it the perfect foil for mauve flowers such as alliums, delphiniums, hyacinths, and sweet peas. Colors and textures are soft and the arrangements informal, with sprays of delphinium buds and half-open alliums as an unusual touch, and garlands of hyacinth bells hung from the ceiling and reflected in mirrors. The furniture is all quite modern, which makes the delicate shapes of the flowers more fragile.

PICASSO LA JOIE 1945
DE VIVRE 1948

Skira

palazzo
grassi

Touches of pale pink soften the series of green and white arrangements in this period room. The delicacy of the shapes and colors suggests the dappled light of a woodland in spring, with Solomon's seal and sprays of white blossom reflected gracefully in the mirror behind. On the mantelpiece, the gleam of antique silver augments the charm of vintage vases and unadorned glass. Scent is incredibly romantic, of course, and it takes only a couple of white hyacinths to fill the whole room with their perfume.

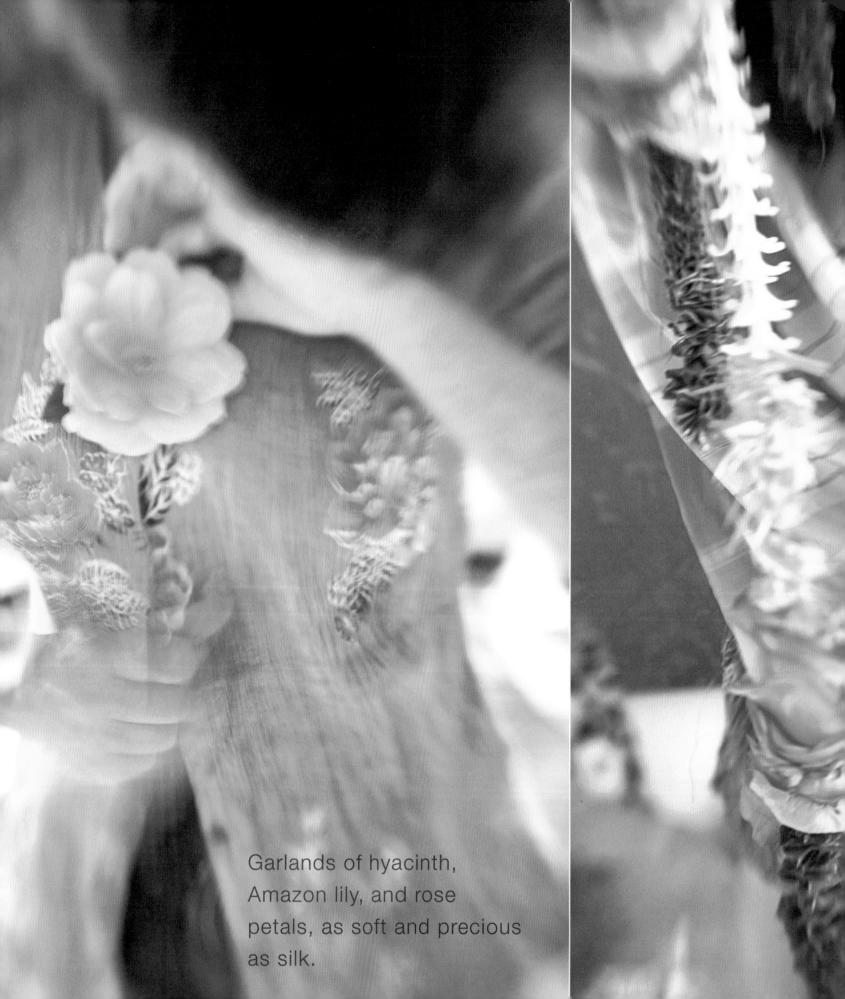

Garlands of hyacinth,
Amazon lily, and rose
petals, as soft and precious
as silk.

Imagine awakening to these beautiful, yet unassuming offerings beside the bed. Pastel pink peonies are lushly luxurious, along with soft half-open rosebuds and a few parrot tulips striped in delicate pinks and milky greens. Vases are small, in plain or colored glass, or pretty pitchers—a couple of blooms even lie in shallow water on an antique majolica plate. The fragility of the flowers only heightens the romantic mood—they are at their fullest and most lovely, poised on the point of decay.

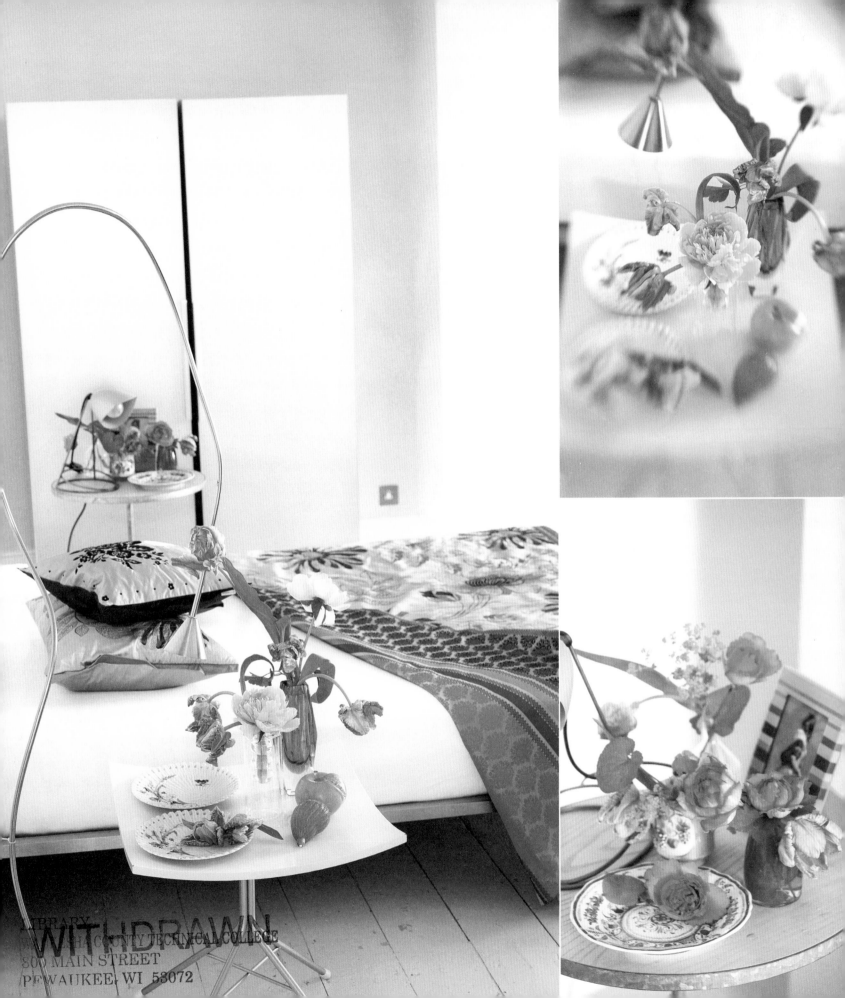

Party

It's easy to buy a big bunch of flowers for a party and leave it at that. But flowers can be used in a multitude of other ways to decorate the whole house in the mood and style of your choice. Wherever you might use paper or other artificial decorations, think of fresh flowers instead. String them in garlands to hang from the ceiling, or suspend from ribbons out of doorways in a fantastic floral canopy. Tie them to chair backs or attach them to presents. Scatter rose petals on tables, or heap them in open bowls. And why use sugared or false flowers on cakes and other desserts when real ones are so much more beautiful? Many of the following are ephemeral creations that take time and effort to produce, but their life-enhancing beauty, shared by many, is well worth it.

Fresh flowers can make an attractive alternative to traditional Christmas decorations. Long-lasting flowers, such as carnations, can be strung in bright garlands (using clear plastic fishing line and lengths of frayed silk fabric) or attached to the branches of a Christmas tree, where the contrast with the deep green needles is fantastic. A daily spray with water keeps them fresh for a good few days.

For a festive tassel effect, string rose petals on clear fishing line with a green snowball like a pompom for the base. (What prettier use for petals when they fall?) And as an alternative to a Christmas tree, place sculptural bare branches in a vase and hang fresh flower garlands, ribbons, and favorite decorations along their length. Red and white are festive colors, especially when teamed with green. And plenty of candles bring the whole look to life.

For a fresh modern take on the Christmas Eve dinner table, choose a green and white color scheme, with seasonal flowers such as scented "Paperwhite" narcissi and sprigs of pussy willow. A centered ceramic vase of white ranunculus, anemones, and Amazon lilies is surrounded by lots of little arrangements in green and clear glass—the large one can be removed before eating to allow your guests to see each other and make room for the food.

As darkness gathers, scattered votive lights illuminate the flowers from below, while tiny white Christmas-tree lights glow softly on the tree outside. The mood is elegant yet inviting, with presents carefully wrapped for each guest. Tucking a few fresh flowers into the ribbon around a present is a lovely little touch that will not be forgotten. Put a few flowers aside when dressing the table—as the gifts are unwrapped they can be added to the little arrangements that sit by each plate. Small gestures such as these take little time and effort but are truly inspiring.

I think of the garden as another room, just outside, and transform it with flowers for a summer party. The central square of pleached lime trees makes the perfect frame for a simple canopy formed by strips of scarlet silk woven in and out between the branches. Just before the guests arrive, pink peonies and dahlias are tied to more silk strips or ribbons and strung like floral pompoms overhead. Cushions, parasols, and even the food are in the same warm, exotic pinks and reds.

Good enough to eat? While some flowers, such as roses and violets, can be crystallized in sugar, others can

be pressed to use as heartbreakingly beautiful cake decorations and simply removed before eating.

For a party in the garden, pick a simple color scheme and stick to it. Here, shades of pink and red—from shell to deepest crimson—sing out against a background of bright green grass. Take a tip from other cultures, and use rose petals to decorate and lightly scent the garden. Heap them in wire baskets, scatter them on old metal tables, and strew them across the lawn. Tie other blooms to chair backs with ribbon and festoon the place with pretty paper lanterns.

Our London garden is again dressed up with fabric and flowers for a party, but with lime green and blues for a fresher daytime feel. Lengths of striped voile form a tent beneath the lime trees, with pretty fabric streamers blowing in the breeze. The same colors are used for the flowers on the table, with bluebells, cornflowers, nigella, and the occasional purple allium pompom arranged simply and unself-consciously in white ceramic pitchers and clear and blue glass. Don't forget to save a flower for your hair!

Country

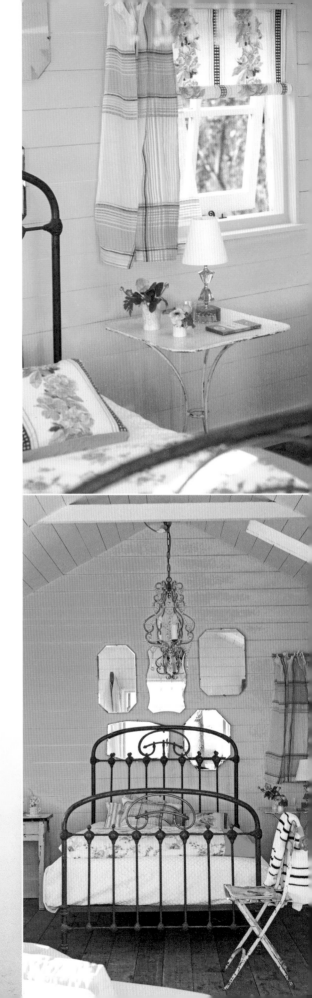

In a country setting, cut flowers need no elaborate arranging or adornment—they are a simple extension of the rural surroundings brought inside the home. Cottage garden favorites such as roses, tulips, and ranunculus, in pretty pastel colors, can be picked fresh from the garden and placed in simple nosegays on bedsides and windowsills. Smaller blooms such as primroses and pansies, which can often go unnoticed in the garden, can be enjoyed at close quarters in simple uncluttered arrangements in vintage cups and saucers. Take color cues from faded floral fabrics or the patterns on old china plates. Sprigs of bright green foliage keep the look fresh and the colors uncloying—experiment with lime alchemilla, feathery fennel, tiny chervil, and textured primrose leaves to contrast with pastel pinks and mauves.

Traditional mixed bunches of flowers can make a large period room, such as this one in a French country farmhouse, seem fussy and old-fashioned. Instead, this spontaneous mix of peonies, alliums, and dahlias in all shades of pink and white are like a breath of fresh country air.

Some stems have been left long, as a nod to the high ceilings and elegant proportions of the room, but a mix of short and tall stems in one vase is a quirky touch that gives the space a modern feel. None of these flowers has particularly attractive foliage, so most has been stripped to leave a strong graphic silhouette. In its place, a few hosta leaves in the same fresh lime green as the cushions and patterned vase weave the whole look together.

Green and white flowers in tiny vases transform an antique tray of pretty scent bottles into a charming tableau. Green carnations, dusky hellebores, papery white peonies, and—unusally—a spray of fragrant elderflower are tucked into little glass vases and bottles in front of the window, where the sunlight can shine through the fragile leaves and petals. A few little florets even adorn the lovely old lace curtains—touches such as these can make a guest bathroom wonderfully welcoming.

I love the opulence of snowballs—their heavy clusters of tiny florets in that unexpected minty green. Native English flowers, which can still be found in country hedgerows, they also make wonderful cut flowers. Here in my London bathroom, they bring the fresh beauty of the countryside to a city setting, teamed with other cottage garden flowers such as lilac, bluebells, hellebores, ranunculus, and a single delphinium spire. Contemporary containers and the artful asymmetry of the arrangements are what give them a modern, urban twist.

The peony print on this wallpaper is so striking that it made sense to bring it to life by filling the room with real flowers in the same rich crimsons, pinks, and white. Though often thought of as cottage garden flowers, peonies have an aristocratic and exotic past, and their opulent frilled petals are at home in any setting. All the color in this

elegant white-paneled room is provided by the flowers and fabric, so it was important to choose flowers that exactly picked out the tones of the furnishings. Ranged on the mantelpiece in antique glass bottles of decreasing size, the lime green leaves of Solomon's seal echo the fresh green of the wallpaper. With its gracefully arching stems and pendant white flowers, this lovely woodland plant should be used more often as a cut flower.

Pansies are so beautiful—I love the way they smile at you. Their lovely patchwork faces can get lost in crowded

arrangements, so I like to use them in simple small-scale nosegays with just a few other garden flowers in shades

that complement their colors. On this bedroom mantelpiece, just a few selected blooms in old glass bottles look much

prettier than one large bunch. The fresh green of scented geranium leaves is the perfect foil for clear pinks and mauves.

Exotic

For centuries, flowers have been our most intense source of color and beauty, and even in this age of digital imagery and mass production their vibrant shapes and colors still have the power to move and amaze. Flowers play a rich part in the religious rituals and everyday lives of people of many cultures. The ancient temples of India are strung with garlands of fresh marigolds, while cows and elephants wander the streets with flowers around their necks. Buddhist monks hold flowers as the focus of their meditations, while in Bali, tiny, intricate offerings of leaves and flowers are made to the gods at certain times of the day. Unconsciously, we are probably doing something similar ourselves as we place a flower on a grave or reverently arrange a vase of blooms on a table or mantelpiece.

Yellow with crimson and scarlet with cerise—these bright, clashing colors bring some of the exoticism of India to this modern London loft. Flowers, whether fresh or on fabric or ceramics, provide almost all the color in this space. Arranged in clustered groups on tables, shelves, and trays, they are almost like offerings on little altars. Some of the tiniest arrangements have the strongest impact: dark carnation heads and scattered rose petals in small metal prayer bowls; sprigs of pink sweet pea in a cup; and a pile of yellow ranunculus and pink carnations.

This garland of orange marigolds, bought from a temple in India and carefully carried home, inspired the creation of many more. Strung on thread or clear fishing line, flowers become something to wear or to festoon around the house. Again, inspired by other cultures, I use flowers to decorate presents—or even make up little floral parcels wrapped in banana leaves and tied with raffia. And when a bunch of roses begins to fade, I scatter the scented petals around the room, pile them in bowls, or float them in water.

Making garlands of fresh flowers is a time-consuming process, but the end result is glorious, so it is definitely worth doing for a party or special celebration. You could even ask friends or family to help—older children love making what are, in essence, grown-up daisy chains. Use thread or fine fishing line, and take care to thread through the thickest part of the flower or bud. Stored in the fridge overnight, then sprayed regularly with water, they should last a few days, depending on the flowers used.

Carnations are not the most fashionable flowers, but they are due for a revival in the style stakes. They come in beautiful, rich colors and last a long time, which makes them good to use in garlands and other decorations where they will be without water for some time. If you are cutting the heads short to float on water in a shallow bowl, gently tear the green calyx at the back of the flower—this frees the petals and allows them to frill out for a looser, more relaxed look.

The fabrics and ornaments in this elegant living room have an Asian feel, echoed and enhanced by the flowers. Pink dahlias and unusual green-tinged roses, such as *Rosa chinensis* 'Viridiflora,' pick out the colors and forms of the beautiful bold prints used to cover the walls and furnishings, with bright green beech leaves and a couple of pink nerines for height. It was well worth taking time to find precisely the right flowers for this scheme. The fabric patterns and little ceramic statues have so much detail that it's important to give them room to breathe, so although the overall look is elegant and sophisticated, the flower arrangements are actually very simple.

Many of the flowers we use each day are exotic in themselves. Although in England we now think of roses and peonies as quintessentially English, all but a few native varieties were first discovered in Asia. The same flowers we buy at the market or pick in our urban gardens may still be growing somewhere wild and unseen on a hillside on the other side of the world. As we appreciate their fragile beauty, they connect us, if we let them, with these faraway places and with the universal truths common to all religions and cultures across the continents and centuries.

118

Minimal

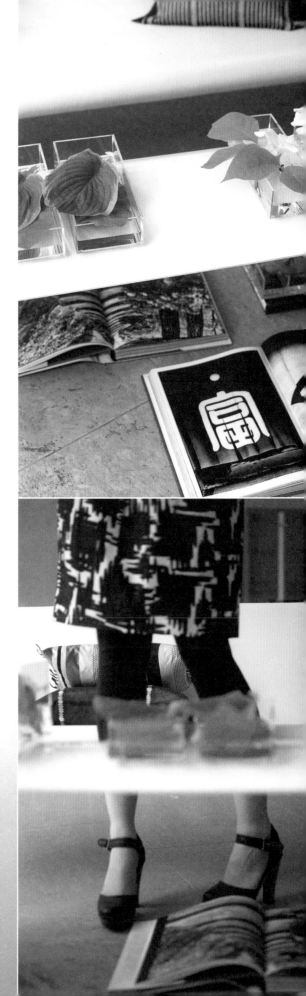

Flowers have a natural opulence and abundance, but used with care and consideration, they can also be strikingly graphic—even minimal at times. It's all a matter of choosing the appropriate blooms, pairing them with the right containers, and editing colors, shapes, and textures down to a minimum. Take time to look at the sculptural forms of different leaves, the intricate geometry of a flower, and the subtly repeating patterns in the sequence of its petals. Some flowers have strong architectural stems, which can be used to great effect; others have a purity of form that needs only a contrasting backdrop to set them off. There are some flowers whose markings have all the intensity of abstract art. Less is often more—though at times a mass or mound of just one flower in a single color can have an amazing impact.

These rows of white flower heads and leaves in low clear Perspex boxes are the perfect complement to the graphic, contemporary style of this room: Three white dahlia heads, a few florets plucked from tall gladiolus stems, and a collection of leaves with strong shapes and textures—nothing more, nothing less. Displaying flowers in unexpected ways enables one to appreciate them with new, more observant eyes. When white is seen on white, all the subtle variations in tone and texture are brought to the fore, with the fresh green of the leaves making an effective foil.

A mass of flowers but one dramatic statement: pink and red peonies and ranunculus heads floating in a sculptural red-lined bowl.

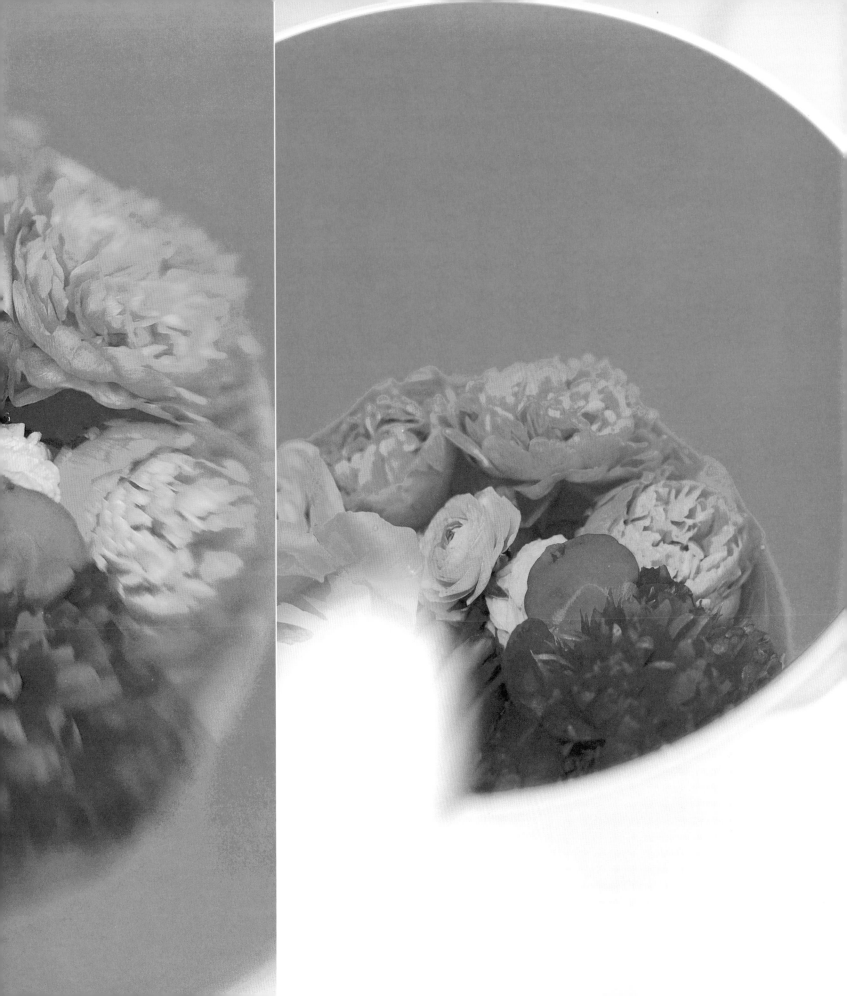

With the perfect partnership of bloom and container, you can sometimes afford to keep things very, very simple. Here, the purity and grace of white Amazon lilies are offset by a glass vase with scarlet lining. In such a pared-down arrangement, the milky green of the unopened buds and darker green of the stems take on extra significance. The fact that red and green are complementary colors only increases the impact—as seen in similar pairings in different white and red vases—some Perspex, some ceramic.

Sculptural arrangements complement the colors and artworks in my green London kitchen. On the table, pink and white peonies, their heads heavy with the weight of their own petals, are lined up in a wedgelike glass vase—country garden flowers made modern by the minimalist container and lifted by winglike leaves on either side. In a further unexpected and spontaneous touch, crimson and white petals of the striped *Rosa mundi* are laid in the boatlike hulls of coconut leaves.

The markings on these oriental poppies are as striking as any Pop Art painting. In their natural state, the flower heads hang down and hide the raspberry-black blotches and beautiful central boss, with its fringe of quivering black anthers. So, instead of displaying them as usual on longer stems, look these gorgeous flowers in the face by cutting the stems short and placing them in narrow-mouthed vases, where they have no choice but to face upward. No further ornament is necessary.

A bold color scheme of black and yellow harks back to the 1950s and perfectly complements the midcentury modern table and the simple shapes of the ceramics. The tissue-paper whorls of ranunculus look as good massed in tiny nosegays as they do on arching graphic stems. Notice how each lemon yellow petal is tinged with orange. Remove the pink camellia and the feeling would become even more minimalist.

Garden

For me, the garden is both a source of wonderful flowers and another space to decorate with them. Some of my favorite flowers—hellebores, with their dusky colors and shy, spotted faces; bluebells; fritillaries; and tiny scented violets—are growing in my own garden, and I love to pick a few to bring into the house or arrange on a table outside. It is almost a cliché now to talk of the garden as an outdoor room, but how many people actually treat their garden as if that were the case, taking care to arrange tables, chairs, and other outdoor furnishings and decorating with fabric and flowers? We have looked at ways to transform the garden for a party, but little everyday touches, such as putting a freshly ironed cloth on a table or cushions on garden chairs and arranging little bunches of flowers here and there, can make a commonplace corner into something truly delightful.

In this sunlit corner, tulips, bluebells, and checker lilies from the garden are mixed with other flowers in soft pinks, mauves, and maroons. The look is spontaneous and informal, using old milk bottles and jars, which focus all attention on the flowers. Bottles are also great for keeping stems in place in the wind. The color scheme is sophisticated, with lime green snowballs, violas, and euphorbia leaves as a contrast; and the artful asymmetry of the arrangements has a quirky, uncommon charm.

Checker lilies can be found growing wild in flower meadows, but their checkerboard patterns, in dark maroon and white, have a sultry, sophisticated beauty, and their shape, when seen in isolation against a clear-colored background, is surprisingly sculptural. Hellebores are another flower not often used for indoor arrangements, but their dusky colors and speckled faces also deserve to be studied at close range. Displayed in simple vases that take only two or three blooms apiece, these flowers can be appreciated for the small living miracles that they are.

Sitting on a balcony off the living room, this small table filled with flowers draws the eye outdoors and helps to merge the house with the garden. The colors—single white peonies, with their golden yellow anthers; lime green alchemilla; and a variegated hosta leaf—have been chosen to complement the impromptu striped fabric awning that has been thrown over the balcony. Simple modern glass and plastic containers in a variety of shapes and sizes echo the contemporary feeling inside the house.

These miniature glass vases are perfect for very small flowers. Walking around the garden, one could pick enough to fill them without anything from the border being missed. What an amazing impact these tiny flowers have, when arranged in this way. A sprig of lavender, a wood anemone, individual hydrangea florets, and a bloom knocked off a delphinium in transit are all given space and attention in this simple celebration of small, unsung flowers.

Smaller, more delicate flowers can get lost against bold patterns, but oriental poppies and peonies can more than hold their own with these striking, retro-inspired prints. Arranging garden flowers inside brings something of the wild abandon and abundance of nature to any room. Opening over several days, these poppies are beautiful in all their parts, from the plump, hairy buds to the frilled and flounced petals to the sculptural central "pepperpot" seedheads, which remain when the rest falls.

Few people think of bringing wisteria indoors, but for those few short weeks when it's at its peak, why confine it to the garden, where it is often seen only from far below? Bring armfuls of the pendulous blooms inside to hang in scented swags and drip elegantly from tall glass vases. The combination of pale mauve flowers and chartreuse foliage is show-stopping, while dark bearded iris are the perfect complement in terms of color and strong, sculptural shape.

Working with flowers

I cannot imagine living without flowers—the repeated rhythms of buying, conditioning, arranging, and rearranging them have become an integral part of my life. Like many other domestic tasks, this can be done quickly and efficiently, without a second thought. But I glean much more satisfaction from lingering over the different stages—from selecting the right blooms for the space and the season to choosing the best container to complement their shapes and colors—and I'm certain the extra time and effort shows in the results. Over the years, I've picked up tips on cutting and conditioning flowers from experts in the field and from my own experience, and am delighted to pass on this wisdom. Well-cared-for flowers not only look lovelier and last longer, they also enhance one's own experience of their brief beauty.

I find that flowers I've grown myself have a radiance and aura about them that is quite unlike those bought from florists. If you have the space, grow your favorite flowers in abundance, so you won't feel bad about leaving a space in the border when you pick them. Or set aside a small patch as a cutting garden. Once the preserve of large country houses, cutting gardens have become fashionable again, and the sight of row upon row of vibrant, brightly colored flowers, just waiting to be picked and arranged, is always a joy.

Caring for flowers

One of the joys of living in London is being able to get up early and go to New Covent Garden Flower Market to buy armfuls of the freshest flowers straight from the stall holders—many of the flowers will have been growing in the ground just a few hours ago. Arriving home with all these treasures to decorate the house for a party is so exciting. One feels like an artist with a new box of paints—the finished picture is not yet clear, but the colors and textures of the raw materials are inspiring.

In the inevitable impatience to start arranging, it is important not to forget to care for the flowers properly. It's not just a matter of dumping them in water and waiting till they die—give your flowers the respect they deserve and they will reward you with a far longer, more vibrant and beautiful life. Many will have come on long journeys—flown from faraway countries, packed in cardboard boxes and wrapped up in cellophane. Like human travelers, they will need refreshing on arrival. And all flowers, even if freshly picked from your own garden, should not be left for a minute without water. Any buckets or large containers will do—tall galvanized florists' buckets not only look good but also help support longer stems as they stand. Fill them one-third full with water—tepid is absorbed better than ice cold. If you want to use flower food, now is the time to add it—the nutrients and antibacterial agents can help the flowers cope with the unnatural conditions indoors.

Conditioning flowers

Stems of store-bought flowers should be recut at this stage—just the bottom inch or two—and ideally at an angle, so that they don't sit flat at the bottom of the bucket and have more of their centers exposed for water uptake. (Professional florists even do this underwater to prevent air locks from forming in the capillary network of the stems.) Woody stems of trees and shrubs, such as the sprays of blossom used on these pages, should have the bottom couple of inches crushed with a hammer (this increases the area for water uptake and prevents a seal from forming). Be sure to use very sharp scissors or hand pruners for cutting, to avoid causing unnecessary bruising.

Softer, sappy stems, such as those of hellebores, poppies, ranunculus, and euphorbia, will benefit from being seared in boiling water—angle the flower heads to prevent them from being scalded by the steam and dip the freshly cut bases in an inch of water for a scant twenty seconds. Then place immediately in tepid water. Searing is worth trying on any flowers that always seem to droop when you try to arrange them inside, particularly garden flowers, which have not been treated by florists. Roses and peonies will also benefit from searing, even if they have drooped already. Cut the stems at an angle first, and they should perk up in an hour or two. If not, soak the entire flower—stems and heads—in a shallow bath of cold water.

The next important task is to remove all the lower leaves from the stems. No leaves should remain below the water line—while being conditioned or within the final arrangement—because they will soon decay to form a bacterial soup, which will not only smell but also shorten the life of all of the flowers in that vase. Stripping the leaves also decreases the demands and stresses on newly cut flowers—leave enough to look attractive, and save the prettiest leaves for other purposes. Some can be added to other arrangements, or used to line clear vases for an unusual touch.

Ideally, the flowers should now be left in their buckets, in a cool place, out of direct sunlight, for a day, or at least overnight. This may be more than your patience can bear, but it is definitely worth doing for a big party or wedding—the flowers will be beautifully vibrant and will last a good few days longer.

Arranging flowers

Preparing flowers in the above way can be a time-consuming job, but it is also a period during which to consider the different blooms and begin to formulate ideas. Place contrasting shapes

and shades next to one another as you work: Would the purple alliums, their spheres of tiny flowers just opening, look better alongside crimson carnations or snowy white peonies? And might those deepest red-black ranunculus look best of all massed in a single bunch on their own? Keep any stray blossoms or buds that fall as you work—they can be charming as part of very small-scale arrangements. It's a source of great satisfaction that so little is wasted—and anything unusable goes straight onto the compost pile.

Choosing containers is a crucial part of the fun of arranging flowers. Don't just go for the conventional option. Along with a huge collection of vases, old and new, I keep pretty old jelly jars and bottles, and also press drinking glasses, Moroccan tea glasses, and vintage cups and saucers into use. Cast out the convention that tall stems go in tall vases and so on—rules are made to be broken; so experiment with your own ideas, and let the flowers lead the way. It's really important to ensure that all your containers or glasses are absolutely clean before you start—even the smallest amount of bacteria will proliferate, with smelly and harmful consequences. Wash them thoroughly in hot, soapy water before you use them. And once you have arranged your flowers, check the water levels every day, especially in hot weather—flowers can guzzle water extremely quickly and will wilt if levels get too low. Change the water altogether at least every other day, checking for spent flowers and leaves as you do so. Have an eye always on what could be reused; if you are removing a delphinium spire because too many of the lower blooms have been lost, save the others for floating on water or showing off in small vases.

When beginning to arrange your flowers, really take time to look at the individual blooms and feel how they might be used to their best advantage. Again, go beyond the usual options; tall stems can look great, but there is nothing to stop you from cutting some of them short—sometimes a flower can be seen in a whole new light by being displayed in an unexpected way. Who says that the stems in a vase should all be roughly the same height? Why not leave some tall, while others can peep over the rim like a floral ruff? In fact, who says flowers need stems at all? Some of the most original arrangements use the heads of flowers nipped off at the top of the stem and floated on water or threaded into garlands on lengths of thread or fine fishing line.

New life for old

Thinking laterally like this is particularly useful when going through an arrangement that is starting to fade. There will be plenty of good blooms that can be given new life in a different arrangement—gladiolius florets can be plucked off the stems, and the small sprays of buds that sprout from the main stems of delphiniums can be used in new ways. It is also a way of redeeming bouquets sent as presents in which too many types of flowers in too many colors have been crammed together with little thought or artistry. Take time to separate out the different types of flowers, perhaps pairing them with others from your own garden or elsewhere. It's hard to think of any flower that isn't beautiful when used in the right way. Some people do not like carnations, for instance—but they come in stunning colors, including white with a raspberry-ripple picotee edge, and are incredibly long lasting. I love to weave them into garlands—they look great with that other fashion outcast, the French marigold—or float the heads in water. Splitting the calyx that holds the petals tightly in place can give a softer look to the flower heads.

Foliage is another area where too much tradition holds sway. Flowers don't have to be teamed with their own natural leaves. Dahlias, for instance, have unremarkable foliage and look far smarter with a few perky lupin leaves. Hydrangea heads look better on their own, but the large textural leaves are good for lining clear vases. And puckered, scrolling hosta leaves, or fresh green spears of violas, can give a lift to almost any arrangement.

When it's time to get rid of your flowers, don't throw roses away. The petals can be strewn on lawns or on the surface of ponds, or dried to make potpourri.

Designers Guild Stockists

Designers Guild lifestyle is available from the Designers Guild Showroom and Homestore, 267-277 Kings Road, London SW3 5EN. Designers Guild fabric & wallpaper is available in the US and Canada through interior designers and architects and can be seen at the showrooms listed below. Your local showroom will be able to give you details of your nearest decorator.

Atlanta
GRIZZEL & MANN
351 Peachtree Hills Avenue
Suite 120
Atlanta, GA 30305
Tel: (404) 261-5932
Fax: (404) 261-5958

Boston
THE MARTIN GROUP, INC.
One Design Center Place
Suite 514
Boston, MA 02210
Tel: (617) 951-2526
Fax: (617) 951-0044
www.martingroupinc.com

Chicago
OSBORNE & LITTLE, INC.
Merchandise Mart – Suite 610
Chicago, IL 60654
Tel: (312) 467-0913
Fax: (312) 467-0996

Cleveland
GREGORY ALONSO SHOWROOM
Ohio Design Center
23533 Mercantile Road – Suite 113
Beachwood, OH 44122
Tel: (216) 765-1810
Fax: (216) 896-9811

Dallas
I. D. COLLECTION
1025 N. Stemmons Freeway
Suite 745
Dallas, TX 75207
Tel: (214) 698-0226
Fax: (214) 698-8650

Dania Beach
AMMON HICKSON, INC.
DCOTA
1855 Griffin Road – Suite B-364
Dania Beach, FL 33004
Tel: (954) 925-1555
Fax: (954) 925-1556

Denver
SHANAHAN COLLECTION
Denver Design Center
595 S. Broadway – Suite 100S
Denver, CO 80209
Tel: (303) 778-7088
Fax: (303) 778-7489

Honolulu
INTERNATIONAL DESIGN SOURCES, INC.
560 N. Nimitz Hwy. – Suite 201E
Honolulu, HI 96817
Tel: (808) 523-8000
Fax: (808) 539-9390
www.idshawaii.com

Houston
I. D. COLLECTION
5120 Woodway – Suite 4001
Houston, TX 77056
Tel: (713) 623-2344
Fax: (713) 623-2105

Kansas City
DESIGNERS ONLY
5225 West 75th Street
Prairie Village, KS 66208
Tel: (913) 649-3778
Fax: (913) 648-8216

Laguna Niguel
BLAKE HOUSE ASSOCIATES, INC.
Laguna Design Center
23811 Aliso Creek Rd. – Suite 171
Laguna Niguel, CA 92677-3923
Tel: (949) 831-8292
Fax: (949) 831-9015
www.blakehouseassociates.com
info@blakehouseassociates.com

Los Angeles
OSBORNE & LITTLE, INC.
Pacific Design Center
8687 Melrose Avenue – Suite B643
Los Angeles, CA 90069
Tel: (310) 659-7667
Fax: (310) 659-7677

Minneapolis
SCHERPING – WESTPHAL
International Market Square
275 Market Street – Suite 209
Minneapolis, MN 55405
Tel: (612) 822-2700
Fax: (612) 822-2332

New York
OSBORNE & LITTLE, INC.
979 Third Avenue – Suite 520
New York, NY 10022
Tel: (212) 751-3333
Fax: (212) 752-6027

Philadelphia
JW SHOWROOM, INC.
The Marketplace
2400 Market Street – Suite 304
Philadelphia, PA 19103
Tel: (215) 561-2270
Fax: (215) 561-2273

St. Louis
DESIGN & DETAIL
2717 Sutton Blvd. – Suite 200
St. Louis, MO 63143
Tel: (314) 781-3336
Fax: (314) 781-3797

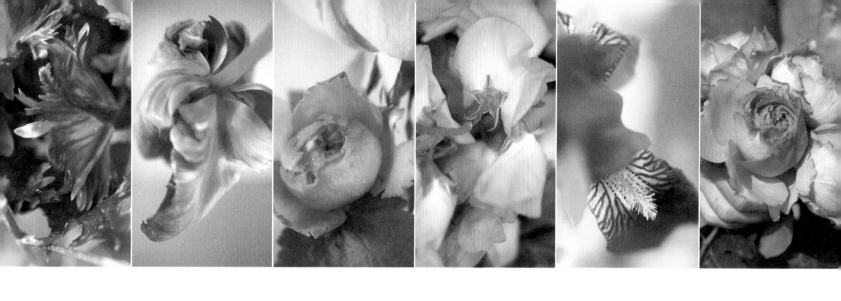

San Francisco

OSBORNE & LITTLE, INC.
101 Henry Adams Street
Suite 435
San Francisco, CA 94103
Tel: (415) 255-8987
Fax: (415) 255-8985

Scottsdale

DEAN-WARREN, LTD.
Arizona Design Center
7350 N. Dobson Road
Suite 135
Scottsdale, AZ 85256
Tel: (480) 990-9233
Fax: (480) 990-0595

Seattle

**THE JOAN LOCKWOOD
COLLECTION, INC.**
5701 6th Ave. S. – #203
Seattle, WA 98108
Tel: (206) 763-1912
Fax: (206) 763-3072

Stamford

OSBORNE & LITTLE, INC.
US Headquarters/Showroom
90 Commerce Road
Stamford, CT 06902
Tel: (203) 359-1500
Toll Free: (877) 322-7420
Fax: (203) 353-0854
www.osborneandlittle.com

Toronto

PRIMAVERA
160 Pears Avenue – Suite 110
Toronto,
Ontario M5R 3P8
Canada
Tel: (416) 921-3334
Fax: (416) 921-3227
www.primavera.ca
info@primavera.ca

Washington DC

OSBORNE & LITTLE, INC.
300 D Street SW – Suite 435
Washington, DC 20024
Tel: (202) 554-8800
Fax: (202) 554-8808

Designers Guild products are available in over 60 countries; for further information please contact our London head office on + 44 20 7893 7400 or info@designersguild.com or visit our website www.designersguild.com

Acknowledgments

Thank you again to our very special team as we work together to create another book: Anne Furniss, Meryl Lloyd, James Merrell, Elspeth Thompson and my very talented creative stylist Liza Giles.

To the team at Designers Guild for their energy and support without whom this book would not be possible, especially: Amanda Back, Helen Burke, Anna Crickmore, Blythe Evans, Lydia Hargrave, Claire Herbert, Ciara O'Flanagan, Liz Poole.

Also thanks to Lucy Merrell, Richard Polo, Marissa Tuazon.

All photographs by James Merrell except pages 22/23, 78/79, 102/103, 140/141, 154/155, 156/157 (1,6,8,9), 158/159 (1,2,3,5,6) by Tricia Guild

First published in the United States of America in 2008 by Rizzoli International Publications, Inc. 300 Park Avenue South, New York, NY 10010 www.rizzoliusa.com

Originally published in the United Kingdom as *Tricia Guild Flowers* in 2008 by Quadrille Publishing Limited Alhambra House, 27-31 Charing Cross Road London WC2H 0LS

Project editor Anne Furniss
Design Meryl Lloyd
Tricia Guild's creative stylist Liza Giles
Production Ruth Deary, Vincent Smith
Typesetting and artwork Keith Holmes redbus

ISBN: 978-0-8478-3130-2
Library of Congress Control Number: 2007934429

2008 2009 2010 2011 / 10 9 8 7 6 5 4 3 2 1
Printed and bound in China

DATE DUE

- 1 MAR 2010

DEMCO, INC. 38-2931